GW00702010

Foreword

Here at the Abbey we dare to say time and again that this is a place where Heaven and Earth Meet.

Five hundred years ago, our modern vision statement found a monumental expression on a West Front that gave pilgrims, monks and the Abbey congregation a glimpse of Heaven from their places on Earth. The exuberant façade must have been a marvel when it was completed and it remains a marvel that still compels people to stop and look and wonder.

The whole front was designed to tell a story to a medieval audience, a story that needs explanation if a modern viewer is to make much sense of it. This booklet identifies characters and suggests several plot lines. The purposes of sculpting apostles, angels and kings are put into an historical context and the hope is that the Abbey front will then be more fully appreciated as a vision of the sacred that retains the power to grip a contemporary imagination. Viewed in its entirety, the west front is too large to take in all at once, too busy to digest within the timescale of a tourist's itinerary. So, another hope is that the text and pictures will draw attention to individual sculptures of great beauty, and provide the information to help bring the particular into focus.

Bath Abbey is beautiful and it is a testimony to faith over many generations. In a world of uncertainty and short-term sensation, the Abbey and its west front have endured. Yet much of what we witness today on the west front is a replacement of what time eroded and a sub-text to this account is that buildings do not and cannot endure fixed and unchanged. Rather, they evolve as their fabric decays and is renewed, and as uses and attitudes shift over time. Nothing created by people is set in stone.

The information in here was scattered among books, architects' reports and within the memories of local people. This is the first time that a west front guide has been assembled into a single document with a key to identify the main components.

The West Front of Bath Abbey invites us to stop and ponder. Do so with this book in hand and walk away enriched.

The Reverend Prebendary Edward Mason

1 Christ in Majesty	14 Virgin Mary	27 Jacob's ladder, north
2 Heavenly host	15 St Andrew	28 Jacob's ladder, south
3 Upper heraldry	16 St John the Baptist	29–34 C19 angels rising
4 Cardinal Castello's coat of arms	17 Unidentified apostle	35 and 36 C19 angels falling
5 Dove	18 Unidentified apostle	37 and 38 C20 angels
6 Henry VII	19 St James the Great	39 and 40 C16 angels
7 Lower heraldry	20 St Matthew	41 Shepherds or Jacob
8 Emblems of the Passion	21 St Philip	42 Shepherds or Jacob
9 Emblems of the Passion	22 Unidentified apostle	43 West door 1617
10 St Peter	23 St James the Less	44 Oliver King or King Athelstan
11 St Paul	24 St Bartholomew	45 William Birde or King Offa
12 Tudor heraldry	25 Bust of St Paul	46 and 47 Oliver King's rebuses
13 St John the Evangelist	26 Bust of St Peter	48 and 49 Pinnacles

The messages

Imagine early 16th-century Bath, its new Benedictine abbey risen vast above a tight urban smudge of wood, thatch and broken Roman stone. Those approaching the city from any direction would have looked for its pristine upper reaches as a landmark and been anxious to move in close to see for themselves the famous west front. Pilgrims – tourists of the Middle Ages – gazed up as we do now at a crowded symmetry, their eyeline drawn to the heavenly host overarching a narrative of saints with their identifying symbols, ladders with angels, devils with scowls, kings with crowns, heraldry and biblical quotations, plus assorted monsters, animals, birds and plants.

What appears to us as severe and inscrutable religious art, with added nifty ladders, was a medieval blockbuster. It is futile to imagine how early-16th-century people experienced the west front, but we can be sure it made more sense to them than it does to us. Instead of the blurred faces and damaged limbs we now look on, they saw sharply carved statues that demanded clear-cut interpretation. They saw a vision of heaven that mirrored their internal pictures of a divinely ordered universe arranged in fixed hierarchies. Everybody knew about angels and prayed to the saints hoping the Virgin Mary, St John the Evangelist or whoever would intercede to spare them from hell and grant entry to heaven.

Medieval Roman Catholicism held that you don't get to heaven through a direct relationship with God. Salvation was gained through the church and the west front's first audience recognised an explicit promise to those who studied its message and then passed through the door. They would have taken the west door as a literal heaven's gate and may well have noticed how the rungs of the heavenly ladders reach down only so far as the *top* of the door. The single mortal elevated to the base of the ladders was Henry VII and thus religious instruction illustrating heavenly access was wrapped up with political spin promoting the new Tudor dynasty's power and authority.

When the Abbey was planned as the centrepiece of a new monastery, Henry VII had only recently taken the throne from Richard III and needed to cement his position. What could serve more obviously to reinforce the earthly hierarchy than showing the top man closer to the angels than anyone else? Henry needed the propaganda because the idea that the king derives the right to rule directly from the will of God must have sat uneasily with the power-grab that had taken place after the Battle of Bosworth Field in 1485. There was also some grateful payback in the Henry homage. Richard III had imprisoned the Abbey's founder, Bishop Oliver King, only for Henry VII to have then released him. The Abbey's affiliations were thus firmly Tudor.

The Abbey, it turned out, was less securely rooted than the new Tudor dynasty. England's last major medieval gothic church was a backward-looking institution, its west front a reactionary statement created at a time when political and religious certainties were unravelling. Henry VII's son Henry VIII declared himself supreme head of the Church of England and the English church broke with Rome. In 1539, not two decades after the west front's completion and with the nave roof still unfinished, Henry VIII dissolved the monastery and vandals moved in. The emerging Protestant conviction of a direct relationship with God rendered the west front's paraphernalia of intercession obsolete and outmoded. Medieval Catholic narratives faded in importance faster than the erosion of soft limestone; that said, we still have enough information to work out much of what it once meant to the people for whom it was intended.

The descriptive route of this guidebook starts with Christ at the top, works down past the dove of the Holy Spirit and then the king who stands above emblems of the Passion. It goes back up through an ascending hierarchy of saints and then down the ladders and out to the aisles and a clutch of more ordinary people. En route are three interpretations. Most popular is a tall tale that would have us believe that the façade is the product of a dream. More credible are two religious interpretations, which differ in emphasis but don't cancel each other out. One interpretation is of salvation through the intercession of saints who were able to pray to God on behalf of those who called on them, the other is of salvation via Jacob's ladder.

THE WRITING ON THE WALL

These words, mostly though not all in Latin, were set in stone for the literate west-front-observer. Most have now faded.

"The key of heaven is made from Simon Peter."
"Behold the fury of Saul is made into the conversion of Paul."

"Every perfect gift is from above."
James 1: 17

"Evil to him who evil thinks."
Motto of the Order of the Garter

"Behold how good and pleasant it is when brothers dwell in unity."
Psalm 133: 1

"My house shall be a house of prayer."
Luke 19: 46

"Trees going to chuse their King said; be to us the Olive King."
Judges 9

Three stories

1. Ten apostles plus the Virgin Mary and John the Baptist

The dozen standing figures either side of the west front are near life-sized statues, which, until recently, were taken to be the apostles. Their original identifying characteristics were fragile stone projections, most of which soon eroded. However, a positive identification of St John (clean-shaven face), St Andrew (X shaped saltire cross) and St James the Great (pilgrim's hat over the right shoulder) made it a reasonable assumption that the other nine figures were the remaining apostles. As there was no standard medieval order of showing apostles, further identification seemed impossible.

Never the less, restorers working with Nimbus Conservation in the early the 1990s gave a fresh interpretation. Earlier repair work had propped the head of sculpture 14 with sloshes of mortar, which were removed to reveal a jewelled crown over long hair that swept into the nape of the neck and behind the shoulder. The face had no sign of a beard and Nimbus Conservation concluded "the likelihood is that ... the most enigmatic of the group ... is intended to be female". It had to be the Virgin Mary. She was, after all, chief among the intercessors to whom the west front's first audience directed their prayers.

The discovery also suggested an ascending hierarchy of saints. "Perhaps," Nimbus reasoned, "their role as intercessors with the heavenly host is being stressed by their proximity to the ground." The diocesan patron St Andrew is with Mary on the first level. So too is St John the Evangelist, who accompanied Mary at the Crucifixion and with whom she is most often depicted. The new attributions also answered an old query about why the upper parts of the front should have duplicated Peter and Paul when they already stand guard, large as life, at the main door.

2. Jacob's ladder

The image of a ladder would have resonated in the medieval consciousness as a loose symbol of hierarchy indicating a top-to-bottom chain of being, a ladder of creation. A more specific understanding of the Abbey's unique west front-feature depends on two quotations. The first, obviously enough, tells of the ladder Jacob dreamed of in Genesis 28:

> Jacob ... stayed that night, because the sun had set. Taking one of the stones of the place, he put it under his head and lay down in that place to sleep. And he dreamed that there was a ladder set up on the earth, and the top of it reached to heaven; and behold, the angels of God were ascending and descending on it! And behold, the Lord stood above it and said,

"I am the Lord, the God of Abraham your father and the God of Isaac." Jacob awoke from his sleep and he was afraid, and said, "This is none other than the house of God, and this is the gate of heaven."ho He called the name of that place Beth el ... saying "this stone, which I have set up for a pillar, shall be God's house; and of all of that thou givest me I will give a tenth to thee."

There is symbolism here embracing God and Mammon, for the story chimes conveniently with the interests of the monks who commissioned the west front and re-established an expensive new Abbey behind it. Jacob said the Church is a gate to heaven named house of God or Beth el. For *Beth* el, read *Bath* and also note the biblical appeal for the tithes which were a main source of income for the Benedictine monks. Remember, Bath Abbey was built as a Benedictine priory. Furthermore, Jacob's story was particularly significant to the founding monks, as outlined in the seventh chapter of the Rule of St Benedict:

> If we wish to reach the highest peak of humility, and to arrive quickly at a state of heavenly exultation ... then that ladder which appeared to Jacob in his dream, on which he saw angels going up and down, must be set up, so that we may mount

by our own actions. Certainly, that going down and up is to be understood by us in the sense that we go down through pride and up through humility. The ladder itself that is set up is our life in this world.

In this final sentence metaphor is presented as reality with a deeper significance than Jacob's dream. St Benedict also considered the pride leading downwards to damnation

Daniel King, 1650s. This first known image of the west front is an illustration from an ecclesiastical survey titled Monasticon Anglicanum. *Judging by the impressionistic sketch, perhaps the artist didn't even visit the Abbey to see it for himself. Aside from the heavenly host and the angels (none of them facing downwards), there is an indifference shown to the sermons being told in the stone.*

and taught his followers that they may go either way. Julian Luxford in an article published in *Religion and the Arts* points to the significance of there being two ladders "the one symbolic of heavenly ascent, while that to the south is equated with descent into hell". He says the Benedictine ladder illustrates the possibility of salvation, the fate of the soul at the last judgement. In 1851, the historian Charles Cockerell noted how the ladder to the heavenly host's left is three rungs shorter than the one to the right and concluded that this indicated the way to hell is shorter.

Other people mention a New Testament ladder story in John 1: 51, which leaves Jacob out of it:

> And Jesus said to him, "Truly, truly, I say to you, you will see heaven opened, and the angels of God ascending and descending upon the Son of man."

3. The dream

The unlikely tale that Bishop Oliver King (1432–1503) saw the west front in a dream first surfaced a hundred years after his death in a story written by Sir John Harington early in the 17th-century. The story is still being repeated uncritically in almost every account of the Abbey. Here is what Harrington wrote:

> Lying at Bathe, and musing or meditating one night late ... [Bishop King] saw, or supposed he saw, a vision of the Holy Trynitie, with angels ascending and descending by a ladder, neer to the foote of which was a fayre Olive tree, supporting a crown, and a voyce that said: "Let an OLIVE establish the crowne, and let a

KING restore the church." Of this dreame, or vision, he took exceeding great comfort, and told it to divers of his friends, applying it to the king his master in parte, and some parte to himself. To his master, because the olive being the emblem or hieroglyfic of peace and plentie, seemed to allude to King Henry VII, who worthly counted the wisest and most peaceable king in all Europe of that age. Thus, though all dreams, be they never so sensible, will be found to hault in some part of their coherence; and so perhaps may this; yet most certain it is (that) he was so transported with his dreame, for the time, that he presently set in hand with this church, and at the west end thereof caused a representation to be graved of his vision of the Trinitie, the angels and the ladder; and on the north side the olive and the crown, with this verse taken out of Judges C9: "Trees going to chuse their King said; 'be to us the Olive King'."

"A poetic invention," wrote Julian Luxford in the journal article where he says Harington's dream was a fund-raising fantasy. Harington implied King's work amounted to God's will in order to elicit the donations to finance the new roof the Abbey still needed. The dismissal of the dream is a preliminary to Luxford's argument that Jacob's ladder – rather than the saints whose iconography his paper ignores – is the west front's defining narrative.

Whether we accept this or not, the west front is more likely an assemblage of familiar scriptural allegories and political signs than the coherent product of an individual imagination, particularly an individual who was asleep. Its authorship is collective, its inspiration corporate and in imitation of earlier west fronts in Wells, Lichfield and Exeter.

John Carter, 1798. The Society of Antiquaries commissioned this illustration before the west front had been amended or restored. The heavenly host is well defined, though some of the climbing angels are eroded. Note that the bottom niche is empty, and that the Tudor heraldry is centred above and below the window as it is today.

The best guess is that sculptors from Lawrence Ymber's workshop carved under the direction of Robert Vertue, the master mason of Bath Abbey and the Henry VII Chapel in Westminster Abbey. Their handiwork, all in the soft local limestone, soon became damaged by the weather, particularly the delicately carved attributes of saints and apostles higher up on the façade and therefore the most exposed to prevailing south-westerly winds.

The stone

A drama other than that of saints and ladders has played out on the west front, for its history reveals shifting attitudes to buildings and their preservation, and to the age-old tensions between repairers and restorers.

The west front was built in a hurry and, when interpreted as a fundamentalist billboard the monastic sponsors of which were going out of fashion, that's not really surprising. Such was the urgency of its religious and political messages that, unusually, it was finished before the nave. When? Most likely is somewhere between Cardinal Adriano de Castello's death in 1518 and 1523. Traces of the cardinal's shields are in the heavenly host and their inclusion suggests the west front was near to completion by Castello's death. A shield in the left aisle window reads 1523 in Arabic numerals.

The names of the west front craftsmen did not really matter at the time, for the renaissance idea of identifying and celebrating individual artists had not quite yet emerged.

THE WEST WINDOW

The stone window frame is a mid-19th-century Gilbert Scott replica of the 16th-century original. The painstaking description below was written in 1798 by John Carter, an architect, illustrator and a master of the long sentence.

"The west window is of extreme richness; it consists of two sub arches and a large division between them, each sub-arch having three divisions, which are likewise seen in the heads of the sub-arches; the spandrels between the heads and the large division in the centre have three divisions, the heights from the bottom of the window to the springing of the arch, have also three divisions, in the heads of the sub-arch. The curious observer must at leisure follow the more minute parts of this mystic architectural design."

While the narrative in stone fell into disrepair – its symbolism of intercession leached of force as it faded from collective memory – the building's fabric was maintained in a patchy way through the 17th and 18th centuries. Then along came confident Victorian improvers replacing roofs, windows and floors and putting in pinnacles and pews. However, they ignored the statues, as had generations of painters, engravers and chroniclers who recorded outline west front views but skimped the details and disagreed about what they saw. For example, the figure at the figure at top of the right ladder (now a bust of St Peter carved in 1900) appears as a grotesque demon in an engraving by John Britton in 1825 while it is recorded as a "saint holding a book" in a 1798 engraving by John Carter (see page 9)

It wasn't until the beginning of the 20th-century that anyone deemed it necessary to revive what had become a ravaged monument. By then, the west front view included GP Manners' pinnacles and George Gilbert Scott's flying buttresses supporting a new stone roof over the nave. Scott also replaced the west window in its entirety and used the scaffolding for the Victorian practice of taking plaster casts of statues. However, Scott's non-intervention with the statues suggests they were still regarded as extraneous items.

In 1899, Canon Quirk was looking for an architect to oversee a west front rethink and he wrote of "carefully avoiding the word 'restoration' and confining himself to the term 'repair'". He hired Sir Thomas Jackson who smartly labelled restorations as repair as he led an overhaul that included sculptures by Sir George Frampton of Christ in Majesty, Henry VII, St Bartholomew and the uppermost eight angels. Jackson didn't touch the heavenly host and voiced a consensus that has held. "I think it better not to renew them, but to leave it to a future generation to do that when the need becomes imperative."

The two main 20th century sculptors are:
• Peter Watts in 1960 (St Matthew, the rebuses, the bottom but one pair of angels)
• Laurence Tindall in 1990 (St Philip)
Tindall was a member of the west front Nimbus Conservation Group team that picked a way through conservation minefields with a delicacy that matched their craft skills. Initial cleaning was carried out with a variety of methods including electronically controlled water sprays, ammonium carbonate poultices, surgeons' scalpels and dental tools. They used a variety of lime mortars to match the colour and texture of the various stones and by taking the Gilbert Scott plaster casts of the carved figures onto the scaffolding, they moved closer to repairing original appearances. Repeated applications of a lime wash applied as a sacrificial coat have helped absorb the worst effects of pollution and weathering. Faintly visible on the edges of stone canopies above statues are metal rods to direct rainwater away and stop birds from nesting on heads and shoulders.

WEST FRONT DATES

Date	Architect/builder	Main sculptor
1499–1523	Robert Vertue	Lawrence Ymber
1539	*Dissolution of the monastery*	
1618	New front door	
1833	GP Manners	
1865	George Gilbert Scott	
1900	Sir Thomas Jackson	Sir George Frampton
1959	Oswald Brakspear	Peter Watts
1992	Nimbus Conservation	Laurence Tindall

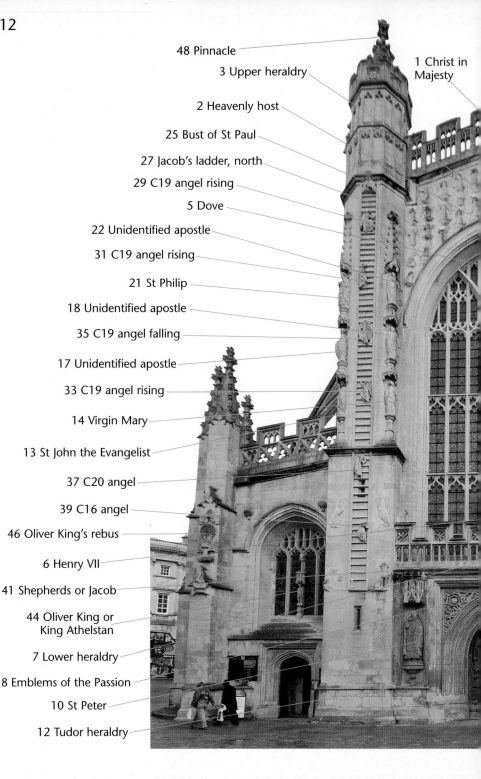

48 Pinnacle

3 Upper heraldry

1 Christ in Majesty

2 Heavenly host

25 Bust of St Paul

27 Jacob's ladder, north

29 C19 angel rising

5 Dove

22 Unidentified apostle

31 C19 angel rising

21 St Philip

18 Unidentified apostle

35 C19 angel falling

17 Unidentified apostle

33 C19 angel rising

14 Virgin Mary

13 St John the Evangelist

37 C20 angel

39 C16 angel

46 Oliver King's rebus

6 Henry VII

41 Shepherds or Jacob

44 Oliver King or King Athelstan

7 Lower heraldry

8 Emblems of the Passion

10 St Peter

12 Tudor heraldry

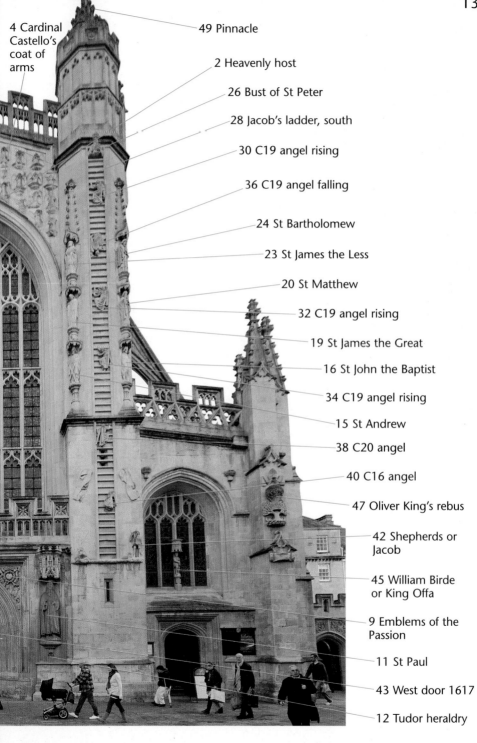

4 Cardinal Castello's coat of arms

49 Pinnacle

2 Heavenly host

26 Bust of St Peter

28 Jacob's ladder, south

30 C19 angel rising

36 C19 angel falling

24 St Bartholomew

23 St James the Less

20 St Matthew

32 C19 angel rising

19 St James the Great

16 St John the Baptist

34 C19 angel rising

15 St Andrew

38 C20 angel

40 C16 angel

47 Oliver King's rebus

42 Shepherds or Jacob

45 William Birde or King Offa

9 Emblems of the Passion

11 St Paul

43 West door 1617

12 Tudor heraldry

Guide to statues and carvings

Christ in Majesty

1 Christ in Majesty, 1900

The west front's focal point shows Christ seated in judgement on a throne, head tilted down on those approaching the Abbey. His right hand is raised with two fingers extended in a salute of blessing and there is a celestial orb in the left hand. The figure is too small for the niche, which was restored in 1865. In 1798, John Carter from the Society of Antiquaries said there had been a representation of the Holy Trinity there "which was once more conspicuous [while] there now only remains a statue of the father". By this account, Christ was above the door where Henry VII now stands. However, in 1899, Sir Thomas Jackson wrote: "The Trinity is usually the seated figure of an old man with a crucifix between his knees and a dove above. I cannot find the slightest trace of this arrangement." Jackson's restoration therefore installed Christ in Majesty at the apex of the west front in a sculpture carved by Sir George Frampton, most famous for his Peter Pan in London's Kensington Gardens.

2 Heavenly host, 1518–23

Revelation 5:11 counted "ten thousand times ten thousand ... angels in a circle around the throne", which is 100 million. Slightly fewer angels flank the throne above Bath Abbey and they are an easily neglected part of what is happening. A modern sensibility looking at these faintly winged stone blobs must appreciate how largely angels figured in the medieval mind. They were messengers who could apprehend God directly and were ranked in nine choirs separated into three orders but what is significant here is their ability to express adoration. This is evident in late 18th and early 19th-century engravings where clearly delineated figures thrust upwards with heads raised and wings curved like brackets around the central figure. What must have been the most dynamic elements of the narrative are now blurred. Nonetheless, "seen from below [they] still have something of their due effect, and a historical interest which new figures, however good, would not possess". So wrote Sir Thomas Jackson, who led the first restoration in 1900.

3 Upper heraldry, 1900

Beneath the main statue is a conglomeration of political and religious imagery. Earthly power is represented in the crowned rose, which Henry VII adopted after defeating Richard III at the Battle of Bosworth Field in 1485 to conclude the War of the Roses. A pair of dogs (Henry VII's white greyhounds of Richmond) flank the crown and they stand above coats of arms for St Peter and St Paul (the Abbey patrons) on the left and St Andrew (the diocesan patron) on the right. Tradition dictated that the left shield should have had a sword for St Paul rather than the bishop's crosier that is actually there. It is difficult to say whether this was a mistake. What we do know is that none of this central upper heraldry is original 16th century carving and that much of the Abbey patrons' coat of arms (though not the crosier) was copied from the main door (see 43 West door below).

Upper heraldry

4 Cardinal Castello's coat of arms, 1518–23

On either side of the crown between the second rows of angels going out from the centre are stone blobs smaller than those around them. They are a pair of shields, details of which are now indecipherable but were recorded by John Carter in 1798, whose "telescope shows them to be charged with two bendlets dexter-embattled and counter embattled surmounted by a cardinal's hat". To those who know, that describes the coat of arms belonging to Cardinal Adriano Castello, the Rome-based absentee Bishop of Bath and Wells from 1503 to 1518. Castello's mention high on the west front suggests that the work was finished by his death. Cardinal Thomas Wolsey, his successor, has no such tribute.

5 Dove, 1960

The dove of the Holy Spirit, wings spread and head lifted, is at the top of the central part of the main window. A dove descended on Jesus' baptism and symbolises purity. An Old Testament dove carried the olive branch that told Noah the Flood was abating and this olive theme links with the rebuses on the aisle fronts. In the mid-19th-century restoration, an uncarved block of stone was included in the upper mullion and there it sat until Peter Watts carved the modern version of a dove in 1960.

The dove

Henry VII and lower heraldry

Emblems of the Passion

6 Henry VII, 1900

A crowned and finely dressed Henry VII stands over the door raised above other men. Above him hovers the dove of the Holy Spirit with Christ's benediction above that. As king, Henry was a minor intercessor and he, like Christ in Majesty, holds an orb in his left hand. Sir George Frampton carved the replacement statue during the 1900 restoration. Some maintain that what preceded Frampton's work was a figure of Christ. Jesus Christ or Henry VII? Church or state? While this is a dispute that will probably remain unresolved, both attributions are credible and the difficulty of interpretation shows the extent to which politics and religion are intertwined on the west front.

7 Lower heraldry, 1900

This was carved in 1900 in a direct copy from earlier engravings of the original 16th-century work. Beneath Henry VII is the Tudor coat of arms supported by the Welsh dragon of Cadwaladr to the left and a greyhound to the right. The shield's fleur-de-lys emphasised an English claim on France (not dropped until 1801) and also represented the Holy Trinity; the three golden lions represent England. The presence of Tudor symbols on the west front might have protected it from monastery wreckers who moved in after dissolution in 1539. As it was, the Abbey was stripped of its glass, lead, bells and ironwork while its stonework was largely left intact.

8 and 9 Emblems of the Passion, 1518–23

The west front's sacred intent is clear in the spandrels (triangles) left and right above the door. They are part of the original message that Christ is the gate to heaven and through His suffering man can enter paradise. The spandrels contain stone-carved depictions of Christ's wounds: the bleeding heart, two pierced hands, two pierced feet, the crown of thorns. At one time the wreath and crown of thorns were green, and the heart, head and feet probably pink. Not surprisingly, the colour from here and perhaps higher on the façade has faded. What is astonishing is that these medieval Catholic symbols of the Passion remained untouched by Puritan zeal. There are also emblems of the Crucifixion above the aisle doors.

10 and 11 St Peter and St Paul, early 1600s

Guarding the gate to heaven and the Abbey's main door are St Peter and St Paul, the two pillars of the Church who are also Bath Abbey's patron saints. St Paul, with his guardian's sword, is to the right. St Peter, the leader of the apostles, is to the left holding a bunch of keys. For those who missed the visual message, Latin inscriptions beneath the statues read: "The keeper of the keys of the gates of heaven is Peter made from Simon" and "Behold the fury of Saul is made into the conversion of Paul." Though taller than the saints above, Peter is shorter than St Paul. He appears hunched up and has no halo probably because the head was lopped off when parliamentary troops used the Abbey as a barracks during the Civil War in 1643. A new face was re-carved into the beard.

12 Tudor heraldry, 1518–23

At ground level, within touching distance (don't), is original early-16th-century Tudor iconography. On the left under St Peter is a Tudor rose and crown and under St Paul is the crown over a portcullis to signify Henry VII's tenuous claim to royal blood through Margaret Beaufort. While the other bits of Tudor heraldry are later additions, these have been there for over 500 years.

13 St John the Evangelist, 1518–23

The young, clean–shaven face of this statue suggests it is St John the Evangelist. The sculpture has its right hand (the only original hand to survive on the west front) held in benediction. St John has a similar elongated face to another St John at the Henry VII chapel in Westminster, suggesting that the original west front craftsman was Lawrence Ymber.

14 Virgin Mary, 1518–23

The Virgin Mary is the main intercessor, the first figure the devout in 1500 would have prayed to for a place in heaven. Until the early 1990s-restoration, it was assumed this figure was an apostle but her identity and the nearby saints makes iconographic sense. The Virgin Mary and John the Evangelist (Jesus' cousin) are usually shown together, as they were at the Cruxifixion. Some perceive a feminine grace to the statue.

St Peter

St Andrew

15 St Andrew, 1518–23

St Andrew is the patron saint of the diocese and therefore has a prime position in the west front's ascending hierarchy. The long-haired and bearded figure has the diagonal X saltire cross resting on his knees and his identification is secure. One foot survives to show a traditional barefoot depiction; the hands, which do not survive, would have held a book. He looks like another St Andrew at the Henry VII Chapel in Westminster.

16 St John the Baptist, 1518–23

Once it was realised the 12 saints were not all apostles, the attribution of the bearded figure on the right of the lower rank was easier. The cloak drawn open to bare the left leg is John the Baptist's traditional indicator and not an attribute of an apostle.

17 Unidentified apostle, 1518–23

The face, the down-turned eyes, the hair and the beard and the finely carved drapery of this early-16th-century original survive but the figure has lost its left arm and shoulder and there are no details to suggest who it is.

18 Unidentified apostle, 1518–23

The statue is tilted towards the prevailing westerly winds and so too weathered to identify. Laurence Tindall, the sculptor who carved St Philip, wrote: "This figure retains overall compositional values in bold sweeps of drapery still defining line and movement and the disposition of form and space."

19 St James the Great, 1518–23

The wide-brimmed pilgrim's hat visible behind the right shoulder identifies this statue. A circular scar could have held the scallop shell which is the emblem of St James' Santiago pilgrimage.

20 St Matthew, 1960

St Matthew was carved during the 1960 restoration. The sculptor was Peter Watts and his work is reminiscent of Eric Gill, under whom Watts studied. As with the St Bartholomew sculpture above it, the identification was guesswork because the originals had become too decayed.

21 St Philip, 1992

St Philip, holding three loaves of bread and a cross, is the newest sculpture on the west front. The original had a fault running through the stone and the upper torso probably fell off in the 1930s. In the early 1990s, the sculptor Laurence Tindall referred to a plaster cast made in the 1860s showing a bearded face though not the attributes. It was carved in the traditional way on an inclined bench so that it is in perspective when viewed from 60 feet below in the Abbey Church Yard.

22 Unidentified apostle, 1518–23

High on the west front and exposed to the weather, this unidentified original is among the most decayed of the figures and no detail of the head remains.

23 St James the Less, 1518–23

The identification of this figure is uncertain but a Victorian plaster cast suggests that the long-haired and bearded statue once held the fuller's club of St James the Less. One of the lower-status apostles, his fuller's club is a tool of the woollen cloth trade and tradition holds he was beaten to death with one.

St Philip

24 St Bartholomew, 1900

St Bartholomew is the patron saint of tanners and bookbinders. He is shown with the flaying knife with which he was martyred and there is a suggestion of older representations that show him with his own skin hanging over his right arm. In his left hand he holds a book. The original of this figure was high up on the most exposed south-west facing part of the west front and was the only replacement apostle from the 1900 restoration.

25 and 26 Busts of St Peter and St Paul, 1900

At the top of each ladder is a bust of one of the Abbey's two patron saints mirroring the two figures by the main door. St Paul is at the top of the left ladder and St Peter at the top of the right. They were carved by Sir George Frampton and installed in 1900. They filled gaps left by a pair of earlier figures possibly of a heavenly welcome on the left and a toothsome devil depicting the mouth of hell on the right.

19th century angel

19th century angel

16th century angel

27 and 28 Jacob's ladder

The ladders, which are unique to Bath's west front, depict a biblical story that was important to the Benedictine monks who founded Bath Abbey. This story and its particular significance is covered on pages 6 to 8. The general significance of the ladders, though, is as straightforward now as it would have been to the first people to crowd in front of the Abbey; these ladders reach upwards towards the afterlife. They do not, however, rest on the ground because the original message was that the route to heaven was strictly through the church. Sir Nikolaus Pevsner's guide to Bath architecture noted that the "church is throughout quite exceptionally uniform in design". However, symmetry was ignored in sculpted ladders of different lengths with the left ladder having 67 rungs and the right 64. A plausible explanation is that the three fewer rungs on the right ladder (which once had an image of the devil at the top) tell us that hell is sooner and more easily reached than heaven.

29–34 Six 19th-century angels rising, 1900
35 and 36 Two 19th-century angels falling, 1900

There were no cheerily humanoid angels descending the medieval ladder. These eight 19th-century angels are works of Victorian neo-gothic imagination and they have attracted a lot of criticism. A 1948 report written by John Hatton said: "My view is that the decayed remains of the original work are of more value than modern reconstructions based largely on conjecture, and that no attempt should be made to renew any of them. The angels on the ladders are a case in point. Sir Thomas Jackson's renewals are excellent 19th-century work, but they do not bear, and perhaps were never intended to bear any resemblance to the originals. To anyone interested in the medieval representation of the Dream they are distractions, and rather tiresome at that. A 15th-century angel may descend a ladder head first in all innocence: a 19th-century one in a similar position only looks like an acrobat." Nimbus Conservation had this to say in 1991: "The 1900 angels suffer from all the worst points of restoration carving – flattened perspective, rigid form, ludicrous positioning of the heads of the falling angels." They were carved by Sir George Frampton from Clipsham stone imported from Rutland.

34 and 38 Two mid-20th century angels, 1960
These were installed as part of a 1960s restoration and were carved by Peter Watts. He lived until 2002 and in his autobiography, *Chipping From Memory*, Watts recalled his young son Matthew passing the open studio door with a schoolfriend and saying: "There's a man in that block of stone, and my dad's going to get him out."

19th century angel

39 and 40 Two early-16th-century angels, 1518–23
The lowest and therefore least weather-damaged of the original angels are 16th-century carvings whose form is still intact despite having no heads or arms or wings. A conservationist consensus holds that they provide a record, however degraded, of the originals and are a yardstick against which to measure restoration work. And, like the heavenly host at the top of the sculpture, they are beautiful in their current state. For an idea of how the angels once were, look high up at the far end of the church interior by the east window where there is a pair of well-defined 16th-century angels. These interior angels were probably carved by the sculptor responsible for the exterior angels, and they definitely follow the same set of sculpting conventions.

19th century angel

41 and 42 Pairs of figures at the base of each ladder, 1518–23
These worn sculptures are the closest the west front has to a civilian contingent. Four figures stand or lie at either side of the base of each ladder. They were traditionally seen as shepherds, but a more recent idea is that they are a kind of cartoon strip of consecutive Jacobs seen during and after his dream. The imaginative might perceive at the base of the south ladder a pillow Jacob used as an altar. Above the figures are scrolls, which once had the words *De sursum est* ("it is from on high") from James 1: 17, "Every perfect gift is from above." In 1899, Sir Thomas Jackson wrote: "The lower figures by tradition represent shepherds, but are now so far perished that no certainty about them is attainable. Any restoration would be purely conjectural, and would destroy such slight traces of the original work as remains."

16th century angel

The west door

A figure of mystery in the south isle window

43 West door 1617

Medieval religious seriousness is missing from the vain heraldry of 17th-century doors that, none the less, hark back to medievalism in their signs and use of Latin and old French. The oak doors were a gift from Sir Henry Montagu to celebrate his brother, Bishop James Montagu, the Bishop of Bath and Wells from 1608 to 1616. The doors' three shields are versions of the Montagu arms: the lower one is for the family as a whole; above right for the second son (shown by the crescent in the middle); above left for Bishop Montagu (the central flying saucer symbol revealing him to be a fifth son). The St Peter keys and St Paul sword of the bishop's shield are reversed from their customary position with the sword pointing left instead of right. While correct heraldic form was upheld on Montagu's tomb inside the Abbey, the blunder was repeated in the west front's upper heraldry. The carved inscription *honi soit qui mal y pense* (Old French: "Evil to him who evil thinks") confirms that the brother wore the order of the garter. Family pride got a shot of sibling sentiment in the Latin inscription on the scroll, which is a section of the first verse of Psalm 133. *Ecce quam* etc means "Behold how good and pleasant it is …" (and perhaps Sir Henry missed out the rest because he assumed the educated would know the verse finishes) "… when brothers dwell in unity." There's heraldic punning going on in this multilingual door for the repeated three diamonds show a *mont* (mountain) *acute* (steep), which sounds like the Montacute that was anglicised as Montagu. The woodwork was restored in 2001.

44 and 45 Aisle windows and statues, 17th-century

Above the left window is the inscription *domus mea* ("My House") to link with the words *domus oronis* ("House of Prayer) above the right/south aisle window and referring to Luke 19: 46 "My house shall be a house of prayer." In 1611, Bishop Montagu paid for the words to be painted in gold leaf. The two little figures in each window are hard to identify. A 19th-century print shows fashionably dressed men, one holding a scroll and the other a full purse. One story has it that the legal business of the parish not involving money was done in the modern entry porch under the man with the scroll; money matters and distribution of charity were transacted in the exit porch under the man with the money bag. Some identify the figures as Abbey benefactors Bishop Oliver King and Prior William Birde; others reckon they are Bishop John Clerk (d. 1541) and Prior William Holloway (d. 1539); others plump for King Athelstan on the left and King Edgar on the right or Offa or Osric or Baldrick, any of whom might have been linked to the foundation of the 10th-century abbey. For a clue to when the west front was completed, a shield on the central mullion of the left window is dated 1523 in Arabic. This is possibly in tribute to Aderlard, a 12th-century philosopher, who was born in Bath and travelled to North Africa from where he brought back knowledge of Arabic numerals and scientific thought.

46 and 47 Oliver King's rebuses, 1960

It was standard for abbey founders to memorialise their good works and the pair of rebuses (visual puns) commemorating Bishop Oliver King would have been easily comprehended. The olive tree (Oliver and sign of peace and prosperity) has a crown around its trunk (surname and Henry VII) and over each tree (which might also represent the tree of Bosworth Field where Henry VII won the English crown) is a bishop's mitre and two animals. Beneath are eroded plaques, which originally carried the punning founder's motto from Judges 9, in Latin on the north and in English on the south: "Trees going to chuse their King said be to us the Olive King." This referred to the parable of the trees in which a worthy olive tree did not want to be king, and an unworthy bramble did. The two carvings were completely renewed by Peter Watts in 1960.

Oliver King's rebus

48 and 49 Pinnacles

The uppermost spiky bits were added in 1833 and amended in the 1860s. Many people were underwhelmed by the gothic fantasies and, to prove there's nothing new about media hyperbole, the local paper labelled discontents as 'the War of the Pinnacles'. The tops of the octagonal turrets supporting the pinnacles contain carved symbols of those who contributed to 19th-century restorations. The left turret includes the compass and divider symbol of the freemasons, who funded the canopies over the saints below.

Bibliography

Caroe and Partners, *Bath Abbey, West Front*, 1991–92

Carter, John, *Some Account of the Abbey Church of Bath*, Society of Antiquaries, 1798

Forsyth, Michael, *Bath (Pevsner Architectural Guides)*, Yale University Press, 2003

Hatton, John, Report on the Conditions of External Masonry and Recommendations for Treatment, 1948

Hylson-Smith, Kenneth, *Bath Abbey: a History*, The Friends of Bath Abbey, 2003

Jackson, Sir Thomas, Report on Exterior Masonry and Sculpture, 1899

Luxford, Julian, 'In Dreams: The Sculptural Iconography of the West Front of Bath Abbey Reassessed', *Religion and the Arts*, Volume 4, Number 3, 2000

Nimbus Conservation Group, Report on the West Front, 1991

Nimbus Conservation Group, 'Bath Abbey West Front: Apostles, Iconography and Composition', 1995

First published 2010 by:
Paulish Books
8 Clarendon Villas
Bath BA2 6AG

Design: Bob Johnson

Photography: Andrew Desmond

Thanks (but no blame) to: Charles Curnock, Penny Fisher, Tim Jollands, Lucy Rutherford, Roland Symons, Laurence Tindall, John Wroughton

Printer: Ralph Allen Press